Mel Bay's

FUN WITH THE JAWS HARP

MW01012575

By Roy Smeck

The jaws harp, we are happy to say, is enjoying a growing resurgence of popularity in today's music. This delightful, primitive instrument with its unique sound is being played more and more by folk artists and bluegrass bands throughout the country. The jaws harp, being relatively easy to learn to play and extremely low in cost, is truly an instrument for children and adults as well as the professional.

In presenting this text we sincerely wish you many hours of musical pleasure with the jaws harp.

Mel Bay and Roy Smeck

Table of Contents

Study Method For The Jaws Harp 2

Buffalo Gals 4

Hand Me Down My Walking Cane 5

I've Been Working On The Railroad 6

Old Mac Donald Had A Farm 8

She'll Be Comin' 'Round The Mountain . . . 9

The Old Gray Mare 10

The Blue Tail Fly 12

Turkey In The Straw 13

There Is A Tavern In The Town 14

1 2 3 4 5 6 7 8 9 0

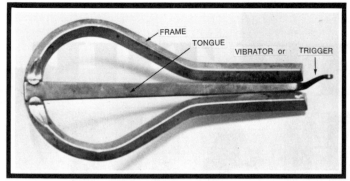

Fig. 1

The Jaws Harp looks like a lyre and it has three parts — the FRAME, the TONGUE and the VIBRATOR or TRIGGER. The length of the TONGUE determines how deep the tone of the Jaws Harp is. Generally speaking the Jaws Harp can play the following tones; the root tone (determined by the length of the tongue), the 3rd, 5th, dominant 7th, and octave.

In addition higher harmonics may be played as indicated by the following music notation:

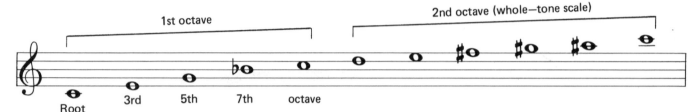

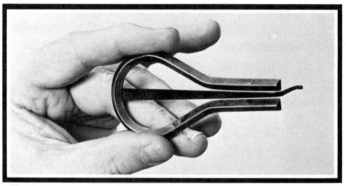

Fig. 2

HOLDING POSITION

Hold the Jaws Harp with the left hand as shown in Figure 2. (If you are left-handed, grasp it with the right hand.) Make certain that the grasp is firm and secure. Make certain that no part of the hand touches the tongue of the Jaws Harp.

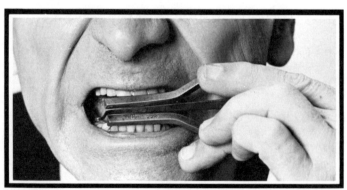

Fig. 3

The vibrator or trigger should point away from the face. Press the upper teeth on the slanting bevel of the upper part of the frame and press the lower teeth similarily against the bevel of the lower part of the frame. See Fig. 3.

If by this time you have tried unsuccessfully to obtain a satisfactory tone, check to make sure:

    A Your tongue is not touching the Harp.

    B Make certain that your left hand is not touching any vibrating part of the instrument.

    C Make certain that your instrument is not defective.

If a buzzing sound occurs when you strike the trigger, it is probably due to the fact that you are pushing the trigger downward or upward. When this is done the trigger buzzes against the metallic frame. Make certain that you strike the trigger horizontally and no buzzing will result.

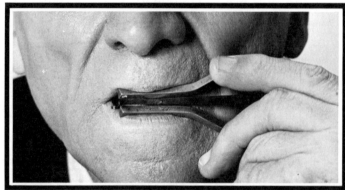

Fig. 4

When the lips are lowered to meet the Jaws Harp, make certain that you do not press too hard against the frame.

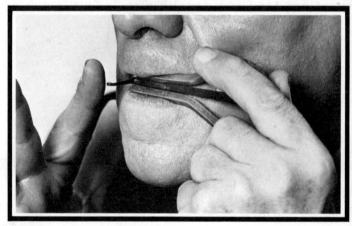

Fig. 5

You stroke the vibrator with the second finger of the right hand. Make all rhythm strokes toward you. Also, to enhance the tone of the harmonics inhale and exhale strongly. See Fig. 5.

TONE QUALITY

In playing the Jaws Harp, the mouth becomes the sound cavity similar to the body of a violin or a guitar. The pitch and depth of the tones produced varies according to the size of the mouth.

To produce low tones draw the tongue as far to the back of the mouth as possible. For higher tones, gradually move the tongue forward.

Practice will show you to what degree you need to move your tongue in order to alter the pitch.

TONE VARIANCE

If you have spent time practicing successfully obtaining different pitches or tones on your Jaws Harp, you are now ready to begin playing the basic sounds produced. The different sounds which can be obtained center around the vowel sounds.

A-E-I-O-U

Strive for *clarity.* Anyone listening to you should be able to understand precisely the vowels you are pronouncing. Try the following exercises:

SYMBOL FOR ONE STROKE OF THE VIBRATOR TOWARDS YOU.

TWO STROKES

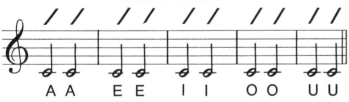

After practicing the vowel sounds try playing the common scale pronouncing as you play:

DO-RA-MI-FA-SOL-LA-TI-DO

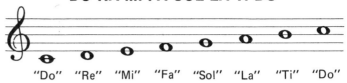

"Do" "Re" "Mi" "Fa" "Sol" "La" "Ti" "Do"

PRONOUNCING SONG LYRICS

A quite interesting effect is obtained when playing a song by pronouncing the lyrics while you are playing. In order to do this you need to practice pronouncing words without moving the lips. In other words you do not move the position of the Jaws Harp when pronouncing a word.

A good way to practice this is to count from 1 to 10 or to say the letters in the alphabet while the Jaws Harp is in place in your mouth.

TRY THE FOLLOWING EXERCISES FOR PRACTICE: TALK THE WORDS

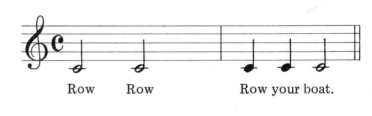

Row   Row   Row your boat.

Good   Night   La - dies.

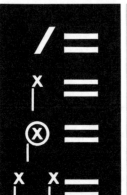

TIME SIGNATURES USED:

4/4 OR COMMON TIME
4 BEATS PER MEASURE, EACH QUARTER NOTE RECEIVES 1 BEAT.

CUT TIME — 2 BEATS ARE COUNTED PER MEASURE.
EACH NOTE RECEIVES ½ ITS NORMAL TIME VALUE.

SYMBOLS USED

ONE STROKE OF THE VIBRATOR OR TRIGGER.

ALSO MEANS ONE STROKE OF THE TRIGGER
EQUAL TIME VALUE (ONE BEAT) TO A QUARTER NOTE.

ONE STROKE OF THE TRIGGER WITH TWO BEATS IN TIME VALUE.

TWO STROKES OF THE TRIGGER WITH TIME VALUE OF
½ BEAT EACH. (SAME TIME VALUE AS EIGHTH NOTES.)

Key of C Buffalo Gals

Key of G Hand Me Down My Walking Cane

Key of G I've Been Working On The Railroad

Key of C Old Mac Donald Had A Farm

She'll Be Comin' 'Round The Mountain

Key of G The Old Gray Mare

Key of C The Blue Tail Fly

Turkey In The Straw

Key of C There Is A Tavern In The Town